THE
COWBOY
AND THE
LION

PEDRO LEON JR.

The Reading Glass Books
1-888-420-3050
www.readingglassbooks.com
fulfillment@readingglassbooks.com

THE
COWBOY
AND THE
LION

THE
JUAN VARGAS
AND
PEDRO LEON
STORY

This story is based on true events that have happened throughout my life, but mostly it's about a boxer by the name of Juan Vargas and I.

I will start this story about my younger years. When I was about seven years old, my mom and dad were divorced. My brothers, sisters and I were split up. My brother Jesse and I were sent to live with my grandparents and uncles in El Centro, CA, and my younger brother Angel and sisters Gloria and Emma were sent to live with our mom in Tulare, CA.

THE COWBOY AND THE LION

My dad lived in a small town about thirty miles north of El Centro in a town called Calipatria. My dad would come and visit us whenever he got a chance, and my brother and I would spend the summers with our mom in Tulare, CA, vice versa for my sisters and younger brother; this went on for many years.

I started grammar school in El Centro, CA, and things were good during those years, first grade through sixth grade. Then, I started seventh grade in September of

1967 at Wilson Jr. High School and that's where my problems started.

I lived on the north side of El Centro, out in the country about seven miles from school one way and attended junior high on the south side of town. Things were okay for a few weeks, but once some students from the north side of El Centro who were attending Kennedy Jr. High that was on the north side of town found out that I was attending Wilson Jr., they became aggressive toward me.

In some cases, I had to fight them off on my way to school and from school at least three times a month, but what they didn't know was that I was watching The Green Hornet on TV with Bruce Lee. I would mimic his moves, kicking, punching, and it sure came in handy as I started to fight off those kids and it worked.

One day, one of my uncles and I rode up to a gas station to air up our tires on our bikes, and as we were airing up our tires, a group of about five kids rode up in bikes and started to harass us. This one big fat kid got off his bike and came at me saying that I was the kid that was going to Wilson Jr. High.

I said, "Yeah, it's me." So as he came at me, I punched him in the face and kicked him in the groin. Then the other kids got off their bikes and also came at me, but remembering what Bruce Lee would do, I would do it. I started to punch anyone around me after they backed off. I turned around looking for my uncle who was long gone. So I just got on my bike and took off. They followed me for a while, but couldn't catch up to me.

When I got home, I asked my uncle,

"Why did you leave me?" He said that he came for help. Yeah, right! Then came Monday, those kids were waiting for me on my way to school, so again I had to fight my way to school. This went on for a while to and from school, and no one was there for me.

I would get in trouble for being late to school, then I would get in trouble for getting home late. It was a no-win situation for me, and I was just twelve years old, and it was just October of 1967.

There were still more fights to come. I swear there was no end to this. Sometimes, I would go way out of my way to school and from school in order not to fight. Well, 1967 came to an end and 1968 came in, and it was the same thing again, but I was getting a lot better at fighting. I would just pop them in the mouth as soon as they came up to me. After a few weeks into 1968, my fighting seemed to slow down, but I never let my guard down. I had no problems at Wilson Jr. High. For some reason, I was really well liked by all the students at Wilson. Maybe they felt I was like their little brother; I was very thin and still had a baby face.

Summer came along and up north I went with my mom and came back in September, then school started again and I turned thirteen and to the eighth grade I went into, and back to Wilson Jr. High I went.

Just when I thought that there was not going to be any more fighting, how wrong was I. A few weeks into school, again, I was harassed because I was going to school at Wilson Jr. High, and again, I would just pop them in the mouth and off crying and bleeding they went. Again this went on for a few more months. Year 1969 came along and winter break came; that's the only time that I would not get into fights. The new year of 1969 came in. But things remained the same, still being bullied for going to school on the wrong side of town. I was young and naive, and I couldn't understand why this was going on.

One day in late January of 1969, I was surrounded by a group of three kids and about to fight them off when a young man stepped in between us and told the kids to go home. This young man would go and walk his sister to and from school; I would see him off and on to and from school walking with his younger sister. He told me that he would see other kids gang up on me, and asked me why. I told him that's because I was going to a different junior high school called Wilson on the south side of town.

As we walked home, I noticed that he lived across the street from where I lived out in the country. I've seen him before, but I don't recall ever talking to him. On the way home as we talked, he told me to come over to his house so he could give me some boxing tips. I told him that I sure will be there. Then he said, "Okay, I will be waiting for you."

I never knew anything about this young man, just that his name was Manuel. He sure was fast and good on the speed bag. He trained me and taught me well just the basics of boxing. A few weeks after some boxing lessons from him, he told me that he had to go away for a while due to his job. I told him thanks for everything, and he wished me well then gave me a pair of boxing gloves that fitted just perfectly on my hands. I never saw him again.

As kids approached me to fight me, I did exactly what Manuel showed me. One quick jab to the nose, it worked perfectly, that's all they needed. My fights got a little less and less as time went by, but I still continued to train myself. My junior high school was coming to an end and I was very glad that it was.

Once school was over, my younger brother and I went to live with my dad in a small town north of El Centro. We didn't go up north to visit Mom and my siblings anymore. But we stayed in touch via phone.

Thinking that all will be great going to a new school and into high school and no more fights, boy, was I terribly wrong!

High school started in September of

1969, and I was just turning fourteen. Things started out good, I would mind my own business, I met two great guys, Luis and Javier, we kicked it off real good. It's as though we knew each other from another life. We are still friends to this day. I met other guys, cool dudes, but nothing like these two guys. But as the high school year went on and some students found out that I was from El Centro, that's when things started to get nasty.

My first incident happened on the football field. Being a small-town junior varsity and varsity would practice together in football, I was assigned as a defensive linebacker. As the football game was being played, I was under the impression that it would be run in a medium pace. As the play started in a medium run, this one senior student came at me at full speed and got me blindsided and knocked me to the ground on my ass. As I lay there, I'm thinking to myself, WTF just happened to me? Then other teammates ran to pick me up from the ground. Still being in shock, I said to myself, Okay, MF, it's on! Then the other play was coming up, and it was about the same play. But this time, I was waiting for him. Sure enough, he came at me at full speed. As he got close to me, I stepped aside and threw him to the ground. He didn't seem to like it, so he got up and came at me again, but this time we grabbed each other from the face mask. We were then separated by teammates, and I asked this high school senior, "WTF, dude. What's your problem?" He just flipped me off and went back into the huddle. Thinking that it was over, but I was still keeping my guard up. Sure enough, he came back at me at full speed again. I threw his ass into the ground, but this time he got up swinging at me, and I responded with an uppercut to his chin. He then went back in shock and that was it. He never bothered me ever again. That was just the beginning of what was to come. But I was ready.

My next incident happened a few days later when a 250-pound student came into the classroom during lunch as I was resting my head on the desk. This heavy student lifted up the desk and threw me to the floor. I got up from the floor immediately and asked him, "WTF, is your problem?" He then pushed me against the wall and backed off. I then kicked him on his groin; as he bent forward, I began to punch him in his face, and as I was doing this, I felt someone grab me from behind and throw me away. As I was going back, I realized that it was my teacher; he immediately got on my ass and sent me to the office.

As I was sitting at the office, the teacher brought in the heavy student bleeding from the mouth and nose looking for the nurse. The principal then came into the office and talked to the teacher. The principal then called me into his office and asked me, "What happened?" I told him what happened, and I was suspended for three days for fighting. So I was thinking to myself, "Not again!"

I went back to school the following week. My two friends were asking me what happened. I told them what had happened and also what happened at the football field. Before I knew it, my two friends were also being bullied by older guys, who were out of high school, so we started to really really hang out with each other watching out for each other every day during and after school.

All three of us were out-of-towners, but my two new friends were older than I was. I was fourteen, and they were fifteen and sixteen. After that incident with that fat student, I was walking out of the cafeteria when two high school students started to bully me. I've been through this before, so I knew what was about to happen.

One of them said, "What's up, MF?" and I immediately hit that one student in the mouth. Then, his friend went into shock. He couldn't believe what he saw, knowing that I was going to get jumped. I punched the other one in the right side of his face and down he went. Students started to gather around us. That's when my two friends came to my aid, but it was too late, at least they showed up. The teachers, seeing the commotion, ran to our location, and we were escorted to the principal's office for fighting. And again, I was suspended for a few days. Principal didn't want to hear it. So I was screwed again. This was my third fight in three weeks of school, and I still had three years and nine months to go. But I got smart. I started to hang around teachers, not going too far from them. Not even going to the restroom, not that I was scared of anyone. I wanted an education, and to have fun.

A few weeks later, one of my friends gave me a marijuana joint and told me to smoke it. "You will be relaxed."

So I did and I will admit I smoked a joint almost every day during school. I smoked a joint in the morning and at lunch. I was tired of being stressed out sometimes, I would cry out of anger not knowing why I was being bullied, but I stayed strong and never backed off any fight. About a month into school, my friends found themselves a girlfriend, which I really didn't mind, but I was on my own now. No one is watching my back now. So I had to deal with it, but we still hung around together every chance we got. Deep inside of me, I knew there were more fights to come my way, so I had to find the place and time so I wouldn't get suspended from school. So any time I was alone in school, I would go behind the gym; teachers would not wander that far. So after lunch that was my fighting ring. And sure enough, they came like flies of all ages and grades.

I remember one day two brothers surrounded me as I just came out of the cafeteria with a Coke can in my hands not open. One of them said, "What's up, MF?"

I threw my Coke can in between his eyes and punched him in the face. His brother just looked at me and walked away, taking his brother with him. We became friends after that, but I never let my guard down with anyone.

One day during another fight, I noticed this one student that was always lurking around me whenever I got into a fight. I didn't know who this student was, and I really didn't care, but he thought he was a badass with a cigarette always in his mouth.

As 1969 came to an end, I was hoping for a better year. Year 1970 came and the fighting continued, and that one student was always lurking around. And

me going into the office for fighting was almost nonexistent.

One day when I got home from school,

my dad got on my ass about fighting in school. I told my dad that I didn't start the fights and that I was being bullied. He asked me, "Why?"

I told him, "Dad, I wish I knew," and that I had the same problem with students in El Centro.

He said, "Yes, I know about them."

"I don't know what to say, Dad. I have to defend myself." My dad just shook his head.

By April of 1970, things were getting a little better. Some students would get brave and verbal. One night I asked God, "What the hell did I do to you? Don't you have better things to do?" I was mad, and I would cry out of anger. I would ask the students before I beat the shit out of them, "What is the problem? I don't know you, I don't mess with you." I never got an answer. Just a "Fuck you, punk." I was starting to really hurt the students I fought; I needed to teach them a lesson. Then parents started to go to the school and complained about me to the principal. I told the principal they were attacking me; I was just defending myself. That I didn't know why this was going on. The principal told me that I needed to hang around where teachers could see me. I told him that I was already doing that, but that they would stalk me and wait till I was alone. So then I said, "Okay, no problem, I can do that."

It kind of worked; now some students were waiting for me after school, but I would walk with my two friends and their girlfriends every day after school so that kind of worked.

School ended for the summer 1970. I

was happy; the first thing I thought about was no more fighting for three months. Boy, was I wrong again!

My two close friends and I got a summer job doing labor work out in the fields. One day after about three days of working, some guys just started to bully us; they were insulting us and it was on: us three against five. As we were fighting in the middle of the field, the boss drove up and jumped on our ass and fired us right on the spot, and we didn't even get paid for those three days of labor. So we went to my friend's house, smoked a joint, and laughed it off.

Summer came and went very fast, and another school year was beginning. I hoped for no more fights, but again I was wrong. A few weeks into school, I was confronted by a freshman student on my way to class. He asked me, "What's up, ese?" slang for

"What's up, dude?" I told him the sky was up, then he came at me swinging, I just stepped aside and knocked the shit out of him right on the spot. Teachers came out of the classrooms and took me straight to the principal's office. The principal asked me, "What happened?" I told him what had happened and he said, "Okay, Mr. Leon, go to your classroom." I said okay; as I was going to class, that student that I punched was still bleeding from his nose. He just looked at me with watery eyes. Then I asked him, "What's up, ese?" and walked away.

I had no pleasure in hurting anyone, but I had no choice. If I didn't do it right the first time, I knew they would come back for more. And that one student that was always lurking around, he would just stare me down but never said a word to me.

After a while, students and teachers were standing up for me. So the principal called me in again to his office and told me, "I've been hearing about those students that you've been having problems with, but if I can help you, please let me know."

I told him, "It's not like they're going to tell me in advance that they are going to kick my ass. It just happens and I don't want to be known as a snitch."

He said, "Okay," and I walked out of the office.

One day one of the students who was a friend of mine was punched in the face while sitting down in the library. He really got messed up, and I knew who did it. That was the only time during high school that I fucked someone up without notice, and I told him it's payback for beating on my friend, and of course, I was suspended from school again.

Year 1970 came to an end, and 1971 came in. Fights were mostly out of school grounds now, and it was perfect for me, because I couldn't get suspended anymore, but the cops started to get involved. Since this was a small town, everyone knew everyone including the cops, so I was shit out of luck. I'm telling you. Sometimes! Why was he allowing this to happen to me? I'm just a kid. I would tell him he didn't seem to care 'cause fights kept coming my way. Slowing down, but not enough.

I joined a local band for the fun of it thinking it would keep me out of trouble, boy, was I wrong again! It was like open season on my ass; there was no way out. Even the poor band members got involved. Every time we had a gig, sure enough, something was going to happen. I think the haters were just jealous of us. I was only fifteen years old by this time. The school year ended again, so some friends and I went up to northern California to work.

One day while we were working, a young girl was working next to me when all I did was say hi to her. Next thing I know, two of her brothers are on my ass, here we are fighting in the middle of the tomato field, in northern California.

I got fired. There was no hope for me, but I stayed strong. I really had no family to back me up. I was on my own even in El Centro when I was attending junior high. Or in that town where I went to high school. Well, school started again, I turned sixteen, and sure enough, it was all the same again, stupid freshman always wanted to prove themselves and thinking that I was a punching bag. They would come up to me all tough, but very wrong they were, so then I would have to fight their older brothers.

One day after a fight, I was approached by a student that came from the East Coast and asked me why I was always fighting. I told him that I was just defending myself, that I wasn't looking for any fights! He then asked me if I was interested in boxing, that his father was a boxing trainer. I told him that I sure was. He said, "Okay, good, we will train after school every day." I said, "Okay, cool." My two close friends had girlfriends. I'm sure they wouldn't miss me.

Well, in the beginning of my boxing training, my friend gave me lots of good tips and made me faster and better on the speed bag and in boxing, and they taught me everything about boxing. Sometimes

I felt I was his punching bag, but it was well worth it. I really learned a lot from my boxing friend and his father. And it was a big mistake for haters/bullies. I would knock them out quickly, but that student was still lurking around me. By this time fighting got really slow; students were finally getting off my ass.

Year 1973 came in. I was finally able to relax. I could go anywhere without any problems. It was some time in 1973 when one of my friends came to me and told me that a student that was always lurking around me was going to kick my ass. He was telling everyone but me. So one day during a pep rally, I was sitting down with some friends at the high school gym, when that student showed up. As he was standing there, he seemed to be looking for someone, and that someone was me.

We locked eyes, then he raised his head like saying, "What's up?" and I responded back by raising my head. Then, I got up and I went into the boys' gym locker room, and sure enough, he followed me in. Next thing I know, he pushed me and said, "What's up, MF?" That's when I hit him in the mouth with my right fist and then with my left; he went back into the lockers, then he rushed me and tried to tackle me down. I then started to punch his ribs with my right hand, but then he was able to take me down. Then I landed on top of him, then he took a big bite of my left arm. I kept punching him in the face, but he wouldn't let go. I started to punch his groin; after a few punches, he let go. But I kept punching him in the face. After a few minutes of this, what seemed almost forever, we were broken apart by some teachers. As I was stood up by one of the teachers, I could see that the whole boys' locker room was filled with students and teachers. I then went into the restroom to wash up, then that student walked in next to me to wash up also. Then he asked me why I was punching him on his groin.

"'Cause you were biting my arm and you wouldn't let go." Then he raised his hand and I thought that he was going to hit me. I grabbed his face and pushed his head against the wall several times. There was blood all over that wall, then a teacher walked in and escorted us both to the principal's office.

As we were sitting there, the principal asked that student, "How old are you?"

He replied, "Eighteen, sir."

"What grade?"

"Senior, sir," he said.

Then the principal turned toward me and asked me how old I was. I told him "Sixteen, sir."

"What grade?"

"Eleventh, sir," I said.

Then he told me to leave. I never saw that student again in school.

After that incident, I didn't have many more fights, but the damage was done. Cops were always on my back. The school year ended, and another summer came and went. School started again in September on my seventeenth birthday. I told myself this is it, I gotta stay out of trouble so I can graduate in June of 1974.

Years 1973 and 1974 came without many fights—a few insults, but no fights.

I had a few boxing matches in which I was doing well. My trainer was proud of me. He told me that I had come a long way. I said, "Yup, I have.: One day after school, I was just sitting in the park minding my own business, when this car drove up with three guys in it. This didn't look good to me. Two of them walked up to me, and one of them threw a punch at me, but I stepped back, then the other guy threw a punch at me also. I was able to hit him with a left jab, and the other one tackled me down as I was protecting myself from punches to my face. They started kicking me.

As I was lying there, the cops showed up and broke us apart. Then one cop asked, "What's going on here?" I told the cop that I was just sitting here when those two guys showed up and started fighting with me. As luck would have it, they knew that cop.

I was then booked and taken into Juvenile Hall. The judge had a file on me already from the fights that I had in high school.

The judge told me about the Marine Corps or CYA (California Youth Authority). I told the judge, "The Marine Corps, sir." He said okay.

June of 1974, when I graduated at the age of seventeen, the Marines were at my front door, but my dad would not sign the paperwork. So they said, "Okay, we will see you when you turn eighteen."

Sure enough, on my eighteenth birthday, they were at my front door at 0900, and I was on the Greyhound bus by 0930 enroute to LA for some testing and my physical. By 2200, I was on route to MCRD in San Diego, California. On my way to MCRD, I was thinking to myself, no more fights with haters. I'm going to fight to defend this country. I thought things would change. How wrong I was again!

Just three weeks into boot camp, I was confronted by three white recruits from back East in the restroom, and the bad thing about this was that they were ordered to beat me up by one of the white drill instructors. But when he walked into the restroom thinking that I was dead by the beating, what a big surprise for him that I was still standing. Unable to break me, he set me up, and I was sent to the Marine Corps brig for five weeks. I should have been home for the holidays, but instead I was in the brig for no reason. After my time in the brig, I was asked if I wanted to stay in the Marine Corps, and I said yes, so I was sent back to another platoon to continue my recruit training.

I had just turned eighteen years old and

here I was in a man's world. I thought to myself, damn, I should have gone to CYA. But I stood strong and completed my Marine Corps boot camp training.

Yes, there were times that I would cry myself to sleep wondering, "Why was I going through these evil times?"

After graduating from boot camp, the first people I went to visit were my two friends, Luis and Javier. They had married their high school sweethearts (Anita and Juanita). They were so proud of me; one of them pulled out a joint and we smoked it. It was the last time in my life that I would smoke a joint. It was a great day kicking it with my two best friends. We reminisced about our high school days; we couldn't believe all those haters in that small town.

After my two weeks of R&R, I was sent to my duty station in Kahanoe Bay in Hawaii.

Maybe it was God's gift to me for going through hell! But the fights with my fellow Marines were not over. Hate continued to follow me. When I was fighting in junior high and high school, it was mostly Hispanics. Now I was fighting racist white Marines. All this time I thought I was going to fight for this country from foreign enemies, but the enemy was in this country. My own fellow white Marines. I gave them a hell of a fight. Then I joined our local base boxing team. I was knocking Marines and civilians out left and right every Friday night. Come Fridays, when we were not out in the jungle training, I was in the boxing ring. The boxing gym would fill up with spectators.

After I did my time with the Marines, I went home and started a boxing team. There were other boxing teams throughout the Imperial Valley. I had about fifteen kids who would box other kids their age.

After many months of boxing events, I got a call from a local boxing trainer who told me that some world boxing champions were going to be attending one of our boxing events and that they had chosen my town to present themselves.

I was very happy to have them show up at our town; it was a nice day that day. There was food, music, and live boxing, and it was all free. One of the boxers from National City in San Diego County asked me, "How did you get involved in boxing?" I told him my life story, and he was amazed. He then told me that he was in charge of the USA Boxing Team for the 1980 Olympics and that the team would be going to Warsaw, Poland, for some boxing tryouts. He then asked me, "Would you be interested in boxing for us?" I said that I sure would. He then told me okay, good. We then exchanged phone numbers and other information. He told me that as soon as they would come back from Warsaw, Poland, he would be giving me a call. I said, "Great, I will be ready."

After everything was over that day, we said our goodbyes and I wished everyone well in Warsaw, Poland. Since I was still in good physical shape after leaving the Marine Corps, I started to work out more and train harder. Never thought that I would get the chance to box professionally. The opportunity was knocking on my door and I had to take it. Just being twenty-one and freshly out of the Marines, I was still in good shape.

After a few weeks of training, I had come home one evening from training, I sat down in the living room to watch TV. As I was watching TV, a special report came on, saying that all of the USA Boxing Team had been killed in an airplane crash in Warsaw, Poland. My blood ran cold. I felt bad for the boxing team and their families. I had met them all a few weeks ago. I gave up the boxing team and just concentrated on family and working.

In 1983, I became an immigration officer in El Centro, CA. So I started another boxing team and made contact with my old boxing teams. Things were going good; some of my boxing kids made it to the golden gloves. In September of 1994, I was involved in a car accident in which I had to have major back surgery. I had bolts and screws placed on my back fused to my vertebrates and left me in a body cast for almost a year and recovering in a hospital bed. A few days after coming home from the hospital, I ordered a TV for my bedroom. A few days later, after ordering the TV, a young man came into my bedroom, telling me that he was bringing in the TV for the bedroom and asked me, "Where do you want the TV placed?" I told him to go ahead and place it on top of the dresser. Which he did and connected the TV to me.

After he finished placing and connecting the TV, he then asked me, "Where did you get all those boxing trophies?" I told him that I had a boxing team and that I used to box, so they were team trophies and some belonged to my two sons who were also boxing. He then told me that he was ranked number 2 in WBA. I then asked him, "Why are you delivering a TV?" He told me that he was going through depression because of his divorce. I then told him that this was depression, lying in bed in a body cast and that I couldn't do anything for myself. That one day you're walking and running around with your family and now lying in bed with a body cast unable to do anything. That I had to rely on someone to do things for me. I also told him, "You're young, don't let anyone bring you down." He then told me his name, Juan "El Vaquero" Vargas. So I told him, "Glad to meet you, Juan," and he said, "Glad to meet you, Mr. Leon."

After all was said and done, Juan asked me if he could come back and talk to me. As I lay there in my body, I told him that he could come back any time that he liked, that I wasn't going anywhere. Juan came to visit me every day after that. We would have long conversations about life. He wanted to know what had happened to me, and I told him. He seemed very interested in my life. And I would ask him about his life and boxing career. Juan would call me to see how I was doing when he was not able to come and visit me. He would ask me, "Sr. Leon, how are you doing today?" And I would say something just lying down like always.

Many months had passed by until I was finally able to move some. I started to walk about twenty steps a day, but I never gave up. The doctor wanted me in a wheelchair, but I said no. As time went on, I kept getting better and better. Juan was still coming by almost every day after work.

About eight months of just lying there, the doctor told me that it was time for therapy. I went to therapy three times a week—oh man, I was in so much pain. I had to learn how to walk, I had no muscle strength in my legs; I would cry during my therapy sessions and sometimes even my therapist would cry just seeing me in pain. She would just walk out with tears in her eyes.

A few weeks into my therapy session, she was no longer there. I was told that she went to work somewhere else. I said, that's good. About two months into my therapy, I was able to walk more and move around more. I didn't have to depend on anyone to help me get around, but I was still limited to my body movements.

One weekend while I was at home, Juan came by in his jeep and asked me, "Let's go for a ride!"

I said, "Sure, but I can't climb up into your jeep."

He said no problem. He then lifted me up and carried me into his jeep and we were gone. He told me that he was taking me to San Diego to meet his boxing promoter and that he had something to tell me. I said, "Okay, cool." As we were going to San Diego, he told me that he wanted to box again, and that he wanted me in his corner. I told Juan thank you, but that I would not be able to help him out that my body will never be the same again. But I could be around for morale and support. He said that would be great. We went to his promoter's house.

As we were in there, he told his promoter that he wanted to get back into boxing. His promoter got very excited hearing the news. As weeks passed by, Juan started training and I continued my therapy sessions, and I would go to see Juan train after my therapy sessions. As time went on, I got better and better, but still limited. The day of my car accident, I weighed 180 pounds. When I started my therapy, I weighed 280 pounds. I needed to lose all that muscle. So I started to go to therapy three times a week for one hour and half. A few months after, Juan started his training. His first fight was set up in San Felipe, Baja California, Mexico, and I was there to see it happen and he won. His confidence was back. He looked good. It was a long ride home, but it was worth it.

About another month had passed by, and Juan was scheduled for another fight in

Mexicali, Baja California, Mexico, and again he won and I was there. He was looking good. His training was looking good for him, and I continued with my therapy three times a week. Juan would still go and pick me up and take me out for joyrides to the beach in San Diego all over the place. He was doing great, and I was doing good. After about one year of boxing, Juan told me that he was scheduled to fight for a title in martial arts. I was in shock, I said, "Juan! What happened to boxing?"

He told me that he couldn't get a title fight here in the States due to an injury. But he was offered a title fight in kickboxing since he had trained under Chuck Norris many years ago. I told Juan that I wished him the best and then he asked me to go with him to Thailand for his title fight. I told him that I couldn't because I was still recovering from my car accident. But I will be there in spirit.

After we talked for a while, I told him to keep in touch and to let me know before he leaves for Thailand.

A few weeks later, Juan called me saying that he would be leaving the valley and going to Thailand. I wished Juan the best and told him to call me after the fight.

A few weeks later, the fight was on. Due to the time change, I think it was like two in the morning here in California. In the morning, I heard that Juan had won the fight, I was so happy for Juan. He called me a few days later telling me that he was on his way home. I congratulated Juan and told him that I was very proud of him.

Juan and I stayed in touch as always. Then he told me he could no longer fight due to his injuries. I told Juan, "It's okay, Juan, it's not the end of the world. You had many good fights, and you came out a champion at the end. You have nothing to be ashamed of." It took fourteen years for Juan to receive his championship belt from Thailand. But in the end, Juan got what he deserved—a World Champion belt.

After 9-11, I was doing a lot better from my injuries and always on the road working. Juan and I lost contact, but he was always in my mind. I retired in 2006 as an ICE agent. It took me more than fifteen years to find Juan again.

This book has been in the works for over fifteen years. I wanted his permission to complete this book even though I really didn't need it. But he was part of my mental and physical therapy, and I know that one way or another I was his therapy.

God Bless you Champ.
Sr. Leon

In closing I would like to thank my beautiful wife Lupe for her patience with me. I would also like to thank all my family and my fishing friends for all the great time's. I would also like to thank our following people.

My Canadian friends.

Gary and Ann.

Wayne and Mar.

Scott and Gwen.

Loisa and Dan.

Jessie and Tiff.

Keith and Maryann.

Judy E.

We would also like to thank Rio Bend RV and golf course Resort Management and all personnel.

Christerpher Leon.

Stay strong. Love you!

My friends.

Benny Galindo and family.

Luis and Anita Flores And family

Juanita B.

Jesse Gutierrez. SEMPER FI!

Rene Escobedo. RIP

my friend, God Bless.

Compa Eliseo, C. And family.

Cesar Ceja from Selma CA.

Turi and Carla.

My BodyGuard Gerry F.

Rosie and Matthew, New York.

Philip Medina. RIP God Bless.

Gary C. From Tucson AZ.

Hayden S.

Joshua Cochrane.

Met at lake Morena.

Teresa V. Kute Cuts.

Rick and Kathy.

George H. Rio Bend.

John Dominguez. Rio Bend

Compa Danny S.

Gabriel M. and family

Gabriel, H. From Chicago.

Juan Vargas and family.

Luis, L. from El Sarape Restaurant Imperial CA.

Best Chicken En Mole

In the world! Management

And Employees.

David V. Gary Indiana.

Wayne H. aka Eddie.

Alberto and Olivia. Rio Bend.

Stephanie, B. My nail girl.

MaLupes Restaurant. Management and staff.

   Imperial

Ca. Best Abondigas.

Chabelas Restaurant.

In Brawley Ca.

Management and staff.

Best Chabelas.

And last but not least.. Ella Turner for doing an outstanding job! and all personnel from The Reading Glass Books.

"PAIN IS TEMPORY.

GLORY IS FOREVER"

SEMPER FI!

Pedro Leon Jr.

www.ingramcontent.com/pod-product-compliance
Lightning Source LLC
Chambersburg PA
CBHW040848120626
46547CB00001B/84